Environme
A World
of Change

Dona Herweck Rice

Published by Pearson Education Limited, 80 Strand, London, WC2R 0RL.

www.pearsonschools.co.uk

This edition is published by arrangement with Teacher Created Materials, Inc. for sale solely in the UK, Australia and New Zealand.

© 2015 Teacher Created Materials, Inc.

Text by Dona Herweck Rice

22 21 20 19 18
10 9 8 7 6 5 4 3 2 1

British Library Cataloguing in Publication Data
A catalogue record for this book is available from the British Library

ISBN 978 0 435 19466 6

Printed in China by Golden Cup

Acknowledgements
We would like to thank the following schools for their invaluable help in the development and trialling of the Bug Club resources: Bishop Road Primary School, Bristol; Blackhorse Primary School, Bristol; Hollingwood Primary School, West Yorkshire; Kingswood Parks Primary, Hull; Langdale CE Primary School, Ambleside; Pickering Infant School, Pickering; The Royal School, Wolverhampton; St Thomas More's Catholic Primary School, Hampshire; West Park Primary School, Wolverhampton.

The author and publisher would like to thank the following individuals and organisations for permission to reproduce photographs and illustrations:
Photographs
(Key: b-bottom; c-centre; l-left; r-right; t-top; bck-background)
Cover: Front **Shutterstock:** Denis Pepin, Ollyy bck, Back **Shutterstock** : tristan tan, Anneka l.
Alamy Stock Photo: Corey Ford/Stocktrek Images 10b,Steve Bloom Images 16, **Getty Images:** iStock 10-11bck, Susan E. Degginge 9tc.**Science source:** Scott Linstead 3, Dan Guravich 20-21bck, Andrew Rakoczy 22, Tom McHugh 24, **Shutterstock:** DeLoyd Huenink 3bck, David Carillet 4, Iakov Kalinin 4-5bck, Monkey Business Images 5t, Xpixel 5bl, Rangizzz 5br, Dark Moon Pictures 7bck,Willyam Bradberry 6-7bck, Pixel Embargo 7bck, Mr Twister 7br, Sergey Nivens 7bc, Ekkachai 7l, Humannet 8-9bck, 9t, 9b,Givaga 9c, Charlie Edward 11t, Rvenitsa 12-13bck, Eric Isselee 12, Tristan tan 13b, Alysta 14-15bck, Rwin 14-15bck, Damsea 15, Sergey Uryadnikov 17,Ken Wolter 18, TravelMediaProductions 19, Pearl-diver 21, Przemyslaw Wasilewski 22-23bck, Nata-Lia 24-25bck, Chris Humphries 25t, Lefteris Papaulakis 25b, Maggy Meyer 26, Ammit Jack 27, Aaltair 26-27bck, CHAINFOTO24 30-31bck, Zirconicusso 31, Antonsov 8532, **123rf:** acik 6, siim 8. **Getty Image:** Prill/istock.
All illustrations: Teacher Created Materials(TCM).

Note from the publisher
Pearson has robust editorial processes, including answer and fact checks, to ensure the accuracy of the content in this publication, and every effort is made to ensure this publication is free of errors. We are, however, only human, and occasionally errors do occur. Pearson is not liable for any misunderstandings that arise as a result of errors in this publication, but it is our priority to ensure that the content is accurate. If you spot an error, please do contact us at resourcescorrections@pearson.com so we can make sure it is corrected.

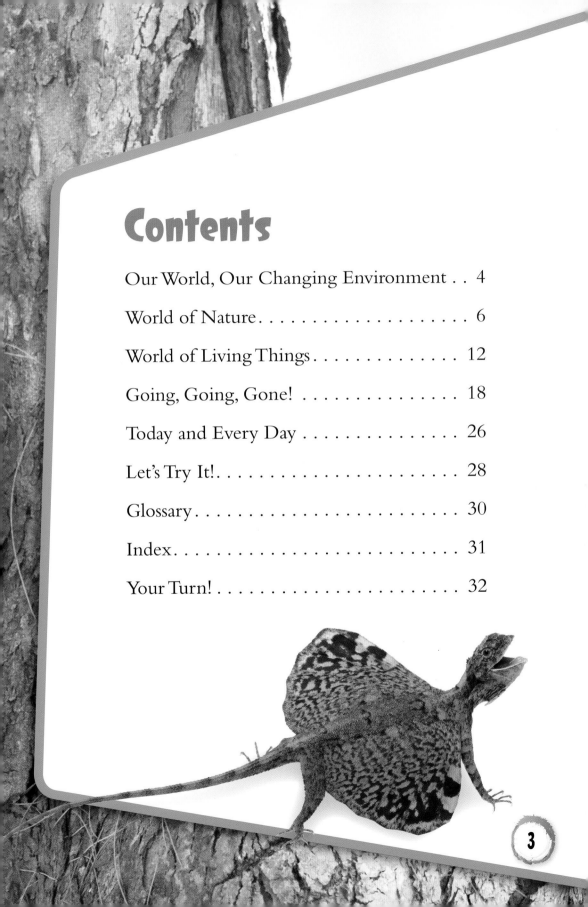

Contents

Our World, Our Changing Environment

The environment is the natural world around us. We can see the environment changing. Sometimes the changes are huge. At other times they are small. Day becomes night. Seeds become plants. Food becomes waste, and you grow up and become an adult!

There are lots of things that affect our world, our environment.

Night turns into day.

Children grow up
and become adults.

Seeds grow
into plants.

World of Nature

Have you noticed how water, land and air are always changing? Every day, as you look around you can see and feel different things about them.

Water changes the land by making it muddy and soft. Over time it can even wear down hard things like rock.

Water cycle

The water in the water cycle is everywhere – on, below and above Earth.

Water

Water is a good example of something that is always changing. On a hot, sunny day, water in seas, rivers and lakes heats up. It turns into steam. The steam rises into the air. As it goes up, it gets colder, and turns back into liquid water. Then it falls on the Earth as rain, hail or snow. When the weather is sunny again, the water heats up and turns into steam again – and so on! This is called the water cycle.

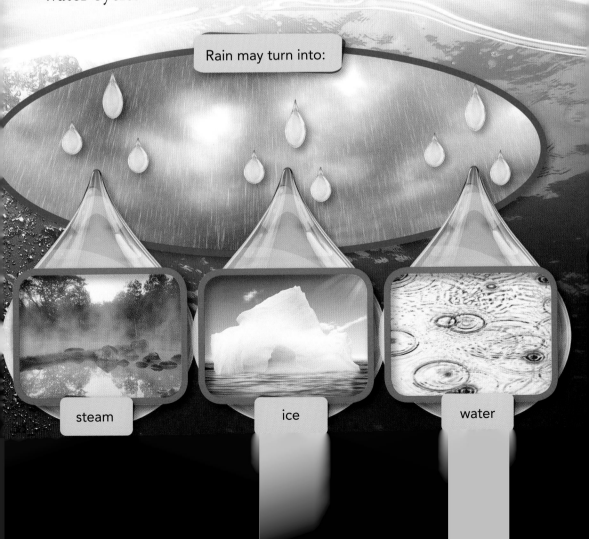

Rain may turn into:

steam

ice

water

Rocks

Rocks seem pretty solid, so it's hard to imagine them changing. But they do change. They break down, and they come together.

Rocks can be broken down bit by bit. It happens through **weathering**. Weathering is the word we use to describe how wind and water break away at rocks. The rocks break down into gravel, sand and dust. These rock bits and pieces, are called sediment. When wind or water moves the sediment, it is called **erosion**.

Rocks also change because of heat and pressure, far under Earth. Some rocks melt below the Earth's surface when they get very hot. Melted rock under the Earth's surface is called magma.

Lava forms when magma erupts from under the ground.

Rock types

There are three types of rock: igneous, metamorphic and sedimentary. Rocks can change from one type to another through cooling, melting, heating and pressure, or weathering and erosion.

igneous

sedimentary

metamorphic

Volcanoes and earthquakes

The top layer of Earth is made of large sections of rock called **plates**. They bump and glide against each other very slowly – at about the same speed as your fingernails grow. We do not usually feel or see this movement. But sometimes people feel it a lot! When Earth's plates move, it sometimes causes an earthquake, or a volcano to erupt.

Stromboli, off the coast of Italy, has been erupting for 2,000 years!

a flooded river in York, Yorkshire, UK

Fires and floods

Fires and floods are a normal part of nature. A fire or a flood can destroy roads, buildings, trees and plants.

World of Living Things

Every living thing on Earth changes too. This is called the life cycle.

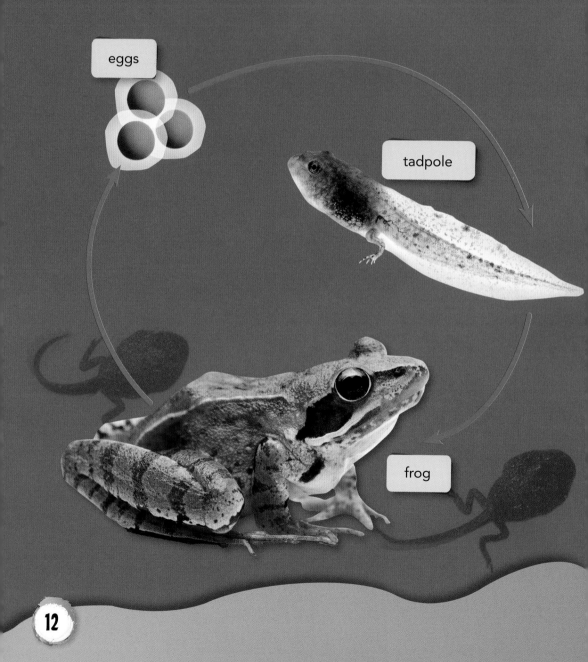

eggs

tadpole

frog

Growing Up

Seeds grow. Puppies grow. Babies grow. All living things start young and new, and grow and grow each day until they reach maturity. Maturity is when living things are fully grown. For people, we call this adulthood.

Even when living things have grown to their full size, they still keep changing. Living things are made of cells, which grow and die all the time. Plants grow new leaves and buds. People grow new skin and hair. As long as they live, living things grow and change.

An oil palm takes three to four years to reach maturity.

Dying

Of course, living things do not live forever. Some live for a short time, such as a mayfly which lives for just one day. Some live for thousands of years, such as yew trees. But everything stops living eventually, because of disease, accident or old age.

When a living thing dies, it decomposes. It decays, or breaks down, and turns into **nutrients** for the soil. The nutrients **nourish** new plants and helps life on Earth continue.

Seagrass

Scientists have discovered seagrass that is more than 200,000 years old!

Every living thing dies.

New life

Death is not the end of the story. New life begins all the time. Plants die, but seeds grow in their place. Animals die, but young animals replace them. People die, but babies are born every day.

These bear cubs will grow up one day.

The cycle of life, death and new life is called the circle of life. The cycle keeps going around and around. As long as living things have the water, food and space they need to live, life continues.

A mother flamingo takes care of her baby chick.

Seals must live near water.

Going, Going, Gone!

A living plant or animal is called an organism. An organism is part of a habitat. An organism's habitat is the area where it lives. It has everything the plant or animal needs to live well.

Penguins need a cold habitat.

The habitat has the right food, water, weather and shelter. The air and water are clean. An organism needs these **conditions** to stay healthy

Sometimes, conditions in habitats change. The weather may get warmer or colder over time. The land may change through plate movement, fire, floods or more. Water sources may dry up. Food sources may go away.

Polar bears have adapted to live in very cold places. They have two layers of fur and ten centimetres of fat to keep them warm.

When a habitat changes, the organisms living there have to **adapt**. This means changing to deal with the new conditions. Otherwise, the organisms must move to a new place. If they do not do one of these things, they will probably die out.

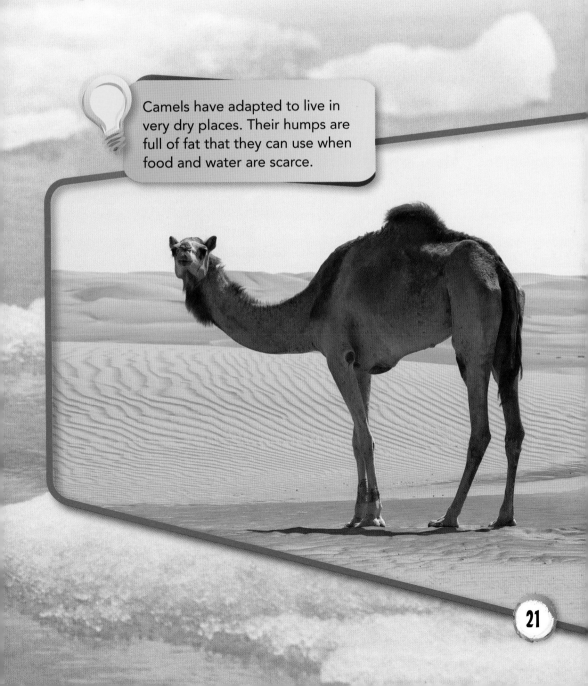

Camels have adapted to live in very dry places. Their humps are full of fat that they can use when food and water are scarce.

Sometimes, it is not nature but people who change a habitat. We pollute the land, water and air. We tear down habitats to build roads, homes and businesses. We introduce plants or animals that do not belong in that habitat, and they may harm the living things that had lived there before.

Coyote concerns

In some places in the USA, coyotes are a problem for people. They may attack and eat pets.

People have invaded the coyotes' habitats and have taken away their food sources but the coyotes are adapting to the new conditions.

As our population grows, we crowd into animal and plant habitats. We take over their homes, and animals and plants may have nowhere else to go.

People cut down this forest. It may have been home to many animals.

When their habitats change, some animals and plants are in danger of not surviving. They become **endangered**. If they are not able to survive, they become extinct. This means they are gone forever.

Flying lizards

A small lizard called a *draco volans* has large folds of skin. These folds let it glide up to 9 metres. This dragon-like animal isn't endangered at the moment, but one day it might be.

Many types of plants and animals that used to live on Earth are now extinct. The most famous of these are dinosaurs. Dinosaurs once ruled the world. Now only their bones remain.

Scientists say that birds may be related to dinosaurs.

Today and Every Day

So, life and planet Earth are always changing. There is birth and growth, death and new life. There is fire and flood and movement, and the landscape changes.

Change is part of life and part of Earth. When we wake up each day, we know that on this day and every day to come, there will be change.

In fact, we can count on it!

Cheetahs are mainly found in parts of Africa.

How do you think this erupting volcano will change the land around it?

Let's Try It!

How do living things change? Try and find out for yourself!

What you need

- ○ fast-growing seeds, such as runner beans
- ○ paper and pencil
- ○ pot with potting soil
- ○ water

What to do

1 Plant a few seeds in the soil, and add water.

2 Put the pot in a sunny place.

3 Observe the pot each day at the same time, and add some water as needed. Draw what you see.

4 Keep observing and drawing daily. What changes do you notice?

Glossary

adapt – change to deal with something new

conditions – the way that things are

endangered – in danger of dying out

erosion – movement of weathered rock and sediment

lava – the hot, liquid rock that flows out of an erupting
volcano

nourish – provide with food for life and growth

nutrients – substances that living things need to live
and grow

plates – large sections of rock in the top layer of
Earth's surface that can move

weathering – the slow breakdown of rock and sediment

Index

Your Turn!

Decomposing fruit

What happens when something decomposes? Watch for yourself. Find an old piece of fruit. Look at it every day. Write about what you see.